Pray Bold Prayers

Bold Prayers that
Crush Fear,
Build Unshakable Faith, and
Unlock the Power of Heaven

Pray Bold Prayers

Bold Prayers That Crush Fear, Build Unshakable Faith, and Unlock the Power of Heaven

By Caleb Elias Hart

Copyright © 2025 LSanders Publishing
All rights reserved.
First Edition

No part of this publication may be reproduced, stored in a retrieval system, or transmitted in any form or by any means including electronic, mechanical, photocopying, recording, or otherwise, without prior written permission from the author, except for brief quotations used in reviews or scholarly works. Pages specifically marked as reproducible within this book may be copied for personal or group use.

Unless otherwise indicated, Scripture quotations are taken from the Holy Bible, New International Version® (NIV®), © 1973, 1978, 1984, 2011 by Biblica, Inc.™ Used by permission. All rights reserved worldwide.

Select Scripture quotations may also be from the Holy Bible, New Living Translation (NLT), © 1996, 2004, 2015 by Tyndale House Foundation. Used by permission of Tyndale House Publishers, Inc., Carol Stream, Illinois 60188. All rights reserved. Cover design, interior layout, and original content © 2025 LSanders Publishing
Published in the United States of America

ISBN: 978-1-968110-05-5

For inquiries: info@LSandersPublishing.com

For more resources, updates, and companion materials, visit:
www.CalebEliasHart.com

Table of Contents

Introduction 3
When Prayer Meets Faith, Heaven Moves 9
    Key Truths: What the Bible Says About Prayer & Faith ... 11
    Examples from Scripture: Faith-Powered Prayers 14
    Barriers to Faith-Filled Prayer 17
    Praying Boldly: Practical Steps to Activate Faith 20
    Bold Prayer: Faith, Rise Within Me 23
Common Prayer Themes 25
Dare to Pray Boldly – Bold Prayers 33
Faith & Confidence 34
Provision and Financial Breakthrough 38
Healing and Restoration 42
Spiritual Growth & Intimacy with God 46
Purpose & Direction 50
Family & Relationships 54
Forgiveness & Freedom 58
Protection & Spiritual Warfare 62
Peace, Rest & Joy 66
Obedience & Discipline 74
Wisdom & Discernment 78
Calling & Ministry 82
Unity in the Body of Christ 86
Identity & Worth in Christ 90

Patience & Perseverance 94

Creative Expression & Kingdom Innovation 98

Time & Priorities 103

Emotional Healing & Wholeness 108

Justice, Mercy & the Marginalized 113

Faith for Generations to Come 118

Conclusion: This Is Just the Beginning 123

Pray BOLD Prayers

21 Prayers That Will Change How You Talk to God and How You Hear from Him

Are you tired of whispering safe, small prayers while your heart is crying out for more?

Pray BOLD Prayers is not a devotional for the timid. It's a 21-day encounter with the power of God through Spirit-led, Scripture-based, faith-filled prayer, written to activate your voice, restore your confidence, and awaken your authority in Christ.

Inside you'll find:

- Bold, focused prayers for healing, provision, breakthrough, purpose, direction, and more
- Scripture meditations will anchor your heart in God's truth
- Reflections help you uncover what's beneath the surface, renew your thinking, and stir your heart toward deeper intimacy with God. What you reflect on today can prepare your soul to receive what God wants to reveal to you today and in the future.
- Faith in Action: These are prompts to use for journaling to make each prayer your own.
- Declaration of Faith and Truth: Speak them with faith. Let them reshape your mindset, fuel your prayers, and steady your walk. Make these declarations to prepare the ground for what God wants to do in you and through you.
- Act of Gratitude, where you can exercise your muscle of being grateful each and every day.
- Overall this is powerful guidance for the most common areas of need in the believer's life

You were never meant to just survive life.
You were created to walk in victory, to stand in boldness, and to pray like you know your Father is listening because He is.

Let us therefore come boldly to the throne of grace, that we may obtain mercy and find grace to help in time of need.

Hebrews 4:16

Whether you need a breakthrough in your finances, restoration in your relationships, clarity for your calling, or strength to keep going, this book will guide you into prayers that shift atmospheres and change lives starting with yours.

You're not just reading prayers.
You're stepping into a lifestyle of bold faith.
Let's pray like heaven is ready because it is.

Introduction

Timid Prayers yield Timid Answers

Have you ever whispered a prayer and wondered if God really heard you?
Have you ever longed to pray with faith that shakes things loose in your life, your family, your future, but didn't know where to start?

You are not alone, and you are not here by accident.

There comes a time in every believer's life when soft prayers and surface-level faith just aren't enough. In such times, you need real answers, real strength, real direction, and you need heaven to respond.

You are invited to step into **bold, Spirit-ignited prayer**. The kind of prayer that moves mountains, breaks chains, and brings clarity where there's been confusion. You are not working towards eloquence or volume because bold prayer is the language of trust. It's what happens when a surrendered heart meets a faithful God.

What You're Holding

Inside these pages are **21 focused and powerful prayers**, each one built on the Word of God, forged in faith, and written to speak directly to the real battles you face. These aren't generic prayers. They are targeted, intentional, and deeply personal.

You'll pray boldly for:

- Healing and restoration
- Financial provision and breakthrough

- Wisdom, direction, and calling
- Relationships and reconciliation
- Discernment, protection, and peace
- Faith to rise, fear to fall, and joy to return

You can use these prayers any time, daily, weekly, or whenever you are troubled or moved. Each prayer theme can be experienced daily and includes:

- A bold prayer to declare and receive
- A Scripture to stand on
- A reflection to stir your spirit
- A journal prompt to process what God is doing
- Declaration of Faith and Truth

Why Bold Prayers?

Timid prayers often flow from timid beliefs. When you believe God is who He says He is, faithful, present, powerful, for you, and much more, then your prayers change and they become confident, specific, fierce, and surrendered.

But without faith it is impossible to please Him, for he who comes to God must believe that He is, and that He is a rewarder of those who diligently seek Him.

Hebrews 11:6

The early Church didn't pray politely.
They prayed with fire, with clarity, and with unwavering trust in the One who still heals, delivers, and provides.

You were made to pray like that.

Pray like that not just in crisis, but in rhythm, in relationship, and in response to the Spirit of God drawing you closer.

What You Can Expect

You may start this book looking for answers, but by the end, don't be surprised if you find **clarity, courage, and closeness with God** that you didn't know was possible.

This is more than a 21-day devotional.
It's a **spiritual turning point.**
It's a training ground for your voice, your faith, and your God-given authority in prayer.

You won't just talk to God, you'll listen.
You'll stand on His Word.
You'll come out stronger, steadier, and more aligned with heaven than when you started.

If your soul has been saying,
"There has to be more…"
then this is it.

If your spirit has been weary,
"I need something real…"
then this is it.

If your prayers have been small,
and your faith has been shaken,
this is your moment to rise.

Open your heart.
Lift your voice.
Let this be the season you stop praying safe and start praying bold.

In faith and fire,
Caleb

Prayer themes

1. Faith & Confidence
2. Provision & Financial Breakthrough
3. Healing & Restoration
4. Spiritual Growth & Intimacy with God
5. Purpose & Direction
6. Family & Relationships
7. Forgiveness & Freedom
8. Protection & Spiritual Warfare
9. Peace, Rest & Joy
10. Hope & Future Promise
11. Obedience & Discipline
12. Wisdom & Discernment
13. Calling & Ministry
14. Unity in the Body of Christ
15. Identity & Worth in Christ
16. Patience & Perseverance
17. Creative Expression & Kingdom Innovation
18. Time & Priorities
19. Emotional Healing & Wholeness
20. Justice, Mercy & the Marginalized
21. Faith for Generations to Come

When Prayer Meets Faith, Heaven Moves

Faith Fuels Prayer

There is a kind of prayer that doesn't just hope, it believes.
A kind of prayer that doesn't just ask, it expects.
A kind of prayer that doesn't beg timidly at heaven's door but knocks with the confidence of a child who knows the door will be opened.

That kind of prayer is called faith-filled prayer, and it moves things.

Faith is what turns ordinary words into divine conversation. It's what transforms your request from a cry of desperation into a bold agreement with God's will. Although faith is necessary as we saw in the earlier scripture, faith doesn't manipulate God, but it activates His promises. It aligns your heart with heaven's truth and gives your prayers weight, authority, and impact.

Jesus never rebuked anyone for having too much faith, only for too little. He constantly connected miracles, answers, and breakthroughs to one thing: Faith.

"According to your faith let it be done to you." (Matthew 9:29)

That means prayer and faith are not meant to be separated.

Prayer is the voice and faith is the fire.

Prayer is the ask and faith is the assurance.

Prayer opens the door and faith walks through it.

When you pray with faith, you stop trying to convince God to do something and start partnering with Him to see His will accomplished.

You don't beg, you believe.
You don't perform, you trust.
You don't wonder if He'll move because you know He is already moving.

If your prayers have felt powerless, stale, or stuck in routine, this may be the missing key: Pray with faith, not a feeling and not a formula, but a deeply rooted confidence in who God is, what He has promised, and how faithful He's always been.

This section is about rebuilding that kind of faith.
The kind that gets your hopes up again.
The kind that makes your spirit stand tall.
The kind that reminds the enemy that you know whose name you pray in.

Because when prayer meets faith, heaven doesn't just listen, it moves.

Key Truths: What the Bible Says About Prayer & Faith

Faith is more than spiritual optimism. It is a powerful, God-given force that activates your prayer life and aligns it with heaven. Without faith, prayer becomes noise. With faith, prayer becomes partnership. These truths anchor your understanding of why faith isn't optional, it's essential.

---

1. Faith Makes Prayer Powerful

"And the prayer offered in faith will make the sick person well; the Lord will raise them up..."
— James 5:15 (NIV)

When prayer is offered in faith, it carries divine authority. This kind of prayer doesn't just speak, it reaches into the spiritual realm and draws down results. James connects faith-filled prayer directly to healing and restoration, reminding us that prayer isn't a ritual. It's a supernatural transaction. The "prayer of faith" is different than wishful thinking. It is a confident declaration rooted in who God is, what He has promised, and what He desires to do, right now.

---

2. Faith Starts Before the Answer Arrives

"Yet he did not waver through unbelief regarding the promise of God, but was strengthened in his faith and gave glory to God."
— Romans 4:20 (NIV)

Abraham praised God before his promise was fulfilled. That's mature faith. Real faith worships while waiting. It doesn't wait for evidence before it believes; it believes because of the One who made the promise. If you wait to feel it before you believe it, you'll miss the power of faith. God is not testing your strength. He's building your trust and trust praises Him as if the answer is already on the way.

---

3. Faith Sees the Invisible

"Now faith is confidence in what we hope for and assurance about what we do not see."
— Hebrews 11:1 (NIV)

Faith gives you spiritual vision, which is the ability to see what isn't visible in the natural. It isn't blind optimism or emotional hype; it's rooted confidence in the unseen realities of God's kingdom. When you pray with faith, you're not guessing. You're seeing through the lens of heaven, trusting that God's promises are more real than your present challenges. You stop being defined by what's in front of you and start being driven by what's been spoken over you.

---

4. Doubt Disrupts Effective Prayer

"But when you ask, you must believe and not doubt, because the one who doubts is like a wave of the sea, blown and tossed by the wind."
— James 1:6 (NIV)

God responds to faith, not uncertainty. Doubt creates instability not because God is unwilling, but because doubt divides your heart. One moment you're praying boldly, the next you're second-guessing. That kind of double-mindedness, James says, makes it hard to receive. The good news is: faith doesn't have to be perfect to be powerful. It just has to be real. Even mustard seed faith, when rooted in trust, can move mountains.

5. Faith Aligns You With God's Will

"This is the confidence we have in approaching God: that if we ask anything according to his will, he hears us."
– 1 John 5:14 (NIV)

Faith isn't about getting God to do what you want; it's about stepping into agreement with what He already wants to do. That's where the power is. Prayer becomes powerful when it's aligned with God's heart, not just our desires. That kind of prayer isn't begging for a breakthrough. It's releasing what heaven already intends. The more you know His will through His Word, the more confidently and effectively you can pray in alignment with it.

Examples from Scripture: Faith-Powered Prayers

The Bible doesn't just teach faith, it **shows** it. Throughout Scripture, we see ordinary people offering extraordinary prayers because they believed God would move. Don't think of these as just stories from the past. These are invitations. The lives of these people show us not only their experiences, written in the Word of God, but also what bold, faith-filled prayer looks like in action.

Hannah: Praying with Brokenness and Expectation

1 Samuel 1:10–20

Hannah was barren, heartbroken, and desperate for a child, but instead of collapsing in despair, she poured out her soul before the Lord. There was nothing elegant or special about her prayer. It was raw, real, and faith-filled. She believed that God not only heard her cry but could do something about it. Even before she saw her miracle, she got up with peace in her heart, because faith had met prayer, and she knew something had shifted.

Lesson: **You don't have to feel strong to pray in faith. You just need to trust that God responds to honest, surrendered hearts.**

Elijah: Praying with Confidence in God's Power

1 Kings 18:36–38; James 5:17–18

Elijah prayed for fire to fall, and it did. He prayed for rain, and after persistent, focused prayer, it came. Elijah's story teaches us that bold prayer isn't about being loud; it's about being confident in the God who answers. The New Testament reminds us that Elijah was a human just like us (James 5:17). The difference? He believed, declared, and didn't stop until heaven moved.

Lesson: **Bold prayers are born from bold faith, the kind that expects fire, rain, or breakthrough, because God is still the same, yesterday, today, and forever.**

The Centurion: Praying with Unshakable Authority

Luke 7:1–10

This Roman officer stunned Jesus when he approached Him. It was not his wealth or position that stunned Jesus, but it was his faith. He believed Jesus could heal his servant with just a word. He understood authority. He related the authority of his command structure to the authority of heaven. It was clear to Jess that he understood it better than many religious leaders. Jesus said, *"I have not found such great faith in all Israel."* And the miracle happened instantly without Jesus even showing up physically.

Lesson: **Faith is not about proximity; it is all about belief. When you recognize the authority in Christ's name, you pray with confidence and receive with bold expectation.**

The Woman with the Issue of Blood: Faith That Presses Through

Mark 5:25–34

Twelve years of suffering, countless doctors, and no answers, but this woman believed that one touch would change everything. She didn't wait for permission or for Jesus to call her forward. She reached out in faith. Jesus said, *"Daughter, your faith has healed you."* Her healing came through bold, risky, personal faith, and her story still moves us today.

Lesson: **Sometimes faith means pressing through the crowd, the fear, and the pain and reaching for the hem of hope.**

Each of these examples carries a unique expression of bold prayer. Whether through silent tears, firm declarations, or desperate persistence, they all had one thing in common: they believed God would move, and He did.

Barriers to Faith-Filled Prayer

What's Keeping You from Praying Boldly?

If prayer is meant to be powerful, why do so many believers feel stuck, hesitant, or unheard when they pray?

The truth is, most people don't struggle with praying, they struggle with believing. Faith-filled prayer is often blocked, not by God's unwillingness to move, but by spiritual resistance inside us.

If left unrecognized, these subtle barriers can weaken your confidence, confuse your spirit, and steal your expectancy.

Here are some of the most common barriers to faith-filled prayer and what to do about them:

---

1. Doubt and Double-Mindedness

"But when you ask, you must believe and not doubt..." – James 1:6 (NIV)

Doubt isn't always loud, sometimes, it's just a quiet voice that asks, "What if God doesn't come through?" Doubt erodes faith by planting questions about God's goodness, power, or willingness to act. Worse still, double-mindedness causes you to pray one thing and expect another. But bold prayer requires a steady heart.

***What to do:* Anchor your faith in God's Word, not your emotions. Faith isn't the absence of questions. Faith is when you refuse to let them lead.**

---

2. Fear of Disappointment

"Hope deferred makes the heart sick..." – Proverbs 13:12 (NIV)

Many stop praying boldly because they've been let down before and disappointment sets in. Unanswered prayers, delays, or loss can leave scars and fear whispers, "Don't get your hopes up again." God doesn't want you to protect yourself from Him. He wants you to trust Him deeper, even in mystery.

What to do:* Be honest with God about your hurt. Then surrender the outcome and declare, *"I trust You, even when I don't understand."

---

3. Unforgiveness and Bitterness

"When you stand praying, if you hold anything against anyone, forgive them..." – Mark 11:25 (NIV)

Unforgiveness shuts down spiritual flow. It hardens the heart and disrupts intimacy with God. Bitterness and offense act like static between heaven and your heart. Faith works through love and love can't thrive in a bitter soul.

***What to do:* Forgive quickly. Release offense, even if they don't deserve it. Free yourself to pray from a clean, open heart.**

---

4. Prayer Without the Word

"If you remain in me and my words remain in you, ask whatever you wish, and it will be done for you." – John 15:7 (NIV)

Praying without knowing God's Word is like shooting arrows in the dark. His promises give direction, power, and authority to your prayers.

Faith comes by hearing and hearing the Word of God (Romans 10:17).

What to do: Make Scripture part of your prayers. Speak His Word back to Him. It will build your faith and sharpen your focus.

---

5. Misunderstanding God's Will

"Your kingdom come, your will be done…" – Matthew 6:10 (NIV)

Some hesitate to pray boldly because they're afraid of praying outside of God's will but God's will isn't a mystery to those who walk closely with Him. His will is revealed through His Word and Spirit.
Remember, praying boldly is not about controlling God; it's about partnering with Him to see heaven manifest on earth.

What to do: Seek His heart first. Then pray with trust and boldness, knowing the Spirit will guide you into alignment.

Do not resolve to the place of shame when you recognize these barriers. This is all about freedom.
Once you see what's been blocking boldness in your prayers, you can tear it down and step fully into the kind of prayer life that flows from faith, not fear.

Praying Boldly: Practical Steps to Activate Faith

You don't need perfect faith to pray bold prayers.
You need real faith. That is the kind that's rooted in who God is, what He has said, and what He still desires to do through you.

Boldness isn't eloquence, volume nor emotion. It's certainty. It's the deep-down conviction that your Father hears you, loves you, and responds when you pray in faith.

Here are five simple, powerful steps to help you start praying boldly today:

---

1. Start with the Word, Not the Need

Let God's promises set the direction for your prayer.
Before you ask, anchor your heart in Scripture. Find what God has already said about healing, provision, peace, or purpose and use His Word as your foundation.

"Your word, Lord, is eternal; it stands firm in the heavens." – Psalm 119:89 (NIV)

---

2. Ask Specifically and Expectantly

Vague prayers get vague results.
Faith prays with precision. Don't just pray, "Lord, help me" but pray, "Lord, give me clarity in this decision," or "Send provision for this exact need."
Be specific, and then expect God to respond in His wisdom and timing.

"You do not have because you do not ask God." – James 4:2 (NIV)

3. Declare the Truth Out Loud

There's power in your words. Don't just think your prayers, speak them.
Declare Scripture. Thank God in advance. Speak life over your situation. Your voice builds your faith and silences fear.

"The tongue has the power of life and death…" – Proverbs 18:21 (NIV)

4. Pray and Stay

Don't rush in and rush out.
After you pray, wait in His presence. Be still. Listen. Let the Holy Spirit speak to your heart.
Bold prayer isn't just about speaking, it's also about listening with expectation.

"My sheep listen to my voice; I know them, and they follow me." – John 10:27 (NIV)

5. Thank God Before You See It

Faith doesn't wait for proof to praise.
Give thanks before the door opens, before the healing comes, before the answer arrives. Gratitude is the evidence of trust. It shifts your eyes off the problem and onto the Provider.

"Do not be anxious about anything, but in every situation, by prayer and petition, with thanksgiving, present your requests to God." – Philippians 4:6 (NIV)

With bold prayer, as any prayer, God answers, but the answer could be yes, no, or not now. You may not get everything you want. It's about walking in everything God has already made available through Christ with faith, confidence, and surrender.

You don't have to wait until you feel bold.
You just have to choose it.

Bold Prayer: Faith, Rise Within Me

Father God,
You are faithful, and Your Word never fails.
Right now, I silence every voice of fear, doubt, and discouragement, and I choose to believe what You have said over what I see.
Let faith rise in me like a fire.
Let every weak place in my belief be strengthened by Your truth.
Let every worn-down prayer be reignited with power.

I don't want to pray safe, small prayers anymore.
I want to pray like I know You're listening because You are.
I want to ask like I know You're able because You are.
I want to believe like I know You're willing because You are.

You said nothing is impossible for those who believe.
So today, I believe again.
I believe You can heal.
I believe You can restore.
I believe You can provide.
I believe You can make a way.

Teach me to walk by faith and not by sight.
Remind me that I don't need perfect understanding to trust You.
Just a surrendered heart and a bold spirit.
And Lord, I surrender now.

Let boldness rise.
Let expectation rise.
Let faith rise within me and never settle again.

In the mighty name of Jesus,
Amen.

Scripture Meditation

"Truly I tell you, if you have faith as small as a mustard seed, you can say to this mountain,
'Move from here to there,' and it will move. Nothing will be impossible for you."
– Matthew 17:20 (NIV)

Reflection: God Honors Even the Smallest Step of Faith

You don't need flawless faith, you just need real faith.
God doesn't require you to have it all figured out.
He simply asks you to believe that He does.

Even the smallest step of faith moves His heart and opens the door to supernatural outcomes.
Faith isn't always loud, but it is always effective.
When you choose to believe, to ask, and to stand, heaven listens, responds, and moves.

Faith in Action

Where in my life do I need to believe God again?
What Scripture can I stand on this week that strengthens my faith and sharpens my prayer?

Declaration of Truth

I declare that faith is rising within me, silencing fear, strengthening my spirit, and unlocking the power of God to move in every area of my life.

Common Prayer Themes

Inviting God into the Realities of Life

As believers, we often return to the same core places in prayer, which are the areas where our hearts long for God to move, guide, heal, and provide.

Every believer will, at some point, face moments of need, desire, and spiritual hunger that call for focused, heartfelt prayer. Some of these moments are personal and quiet, while others are urgent and weighty. Over time, patterns emerge. There are certain areas where many of us regularly find ourselves seeking God's help, wisdom, strength, and direction.

This section brings those places into focus. It outlines fourteen essential categories of prayer that reflect the most common real-life concerns of those walking with God through the everyday and the extraordinary. These include matters of faith, healing, provision, relationships, spiritual growth, and the future, along with areas such as calling, protection, and unity in the body of Christ.

These are essential prayer themes in which followers of Jesus seek clarity, breakthrough, and spiritual strength.

Each topic has been included because it represents a core part of the Christian journey. Whether you are navigating personal decisions, fighting through spiritual battles, or believing for breakthrough and transformation in your family or community, these categories reflect the needs that often stir our hearts the most.

You will find Scripture-centered prayers, reflection points, and prompts for you to journal, which we call Faith in Action, under each heading so you're not left guessing how to pray boldly in the places that matter most.. These are designed to help you connect more deeply with God in the areas where clarity, courage, healing, and breakthrough are needed most. Some of these themes may apply to your life right now. Others may become more relevant in the future.

Use this section as a guide when you don't know what to pray, when you need language for the burden you carry, or when you want to grow stronger in specific areas of your faith.

Let it serve as both a mirror and a compass, revealing what is stirring within you and pointing the way toward God's presence, promises, and power.

Whether you read this in quiet solitude or return to it in a time of pressing need, these prayers can help you speak honestly, trust fully, and keep walking in step with the One who hears and answers.

Let this be your companion as you walk with God through the highs and lows of real life and pray boldly, faithfully, and expectantly in every season. Here is a list of the prayer themes:

Faith & Confidence

- Boldness in prayer and life
- Trust in God's promises
- Courage to obey and take risks
- Freedom from fear, doubt, and double-mindedness

Provision & Financial Breakthrough

- Job opportunities or business growth
- Financial wisdom and stewardship
- Debt freedom and supernatural supply
- God's blessing over home, work, and resources

Healing & Restoration

- Physical healing
- Emotional and mental wellness
- Deliverance from anxiety or depression
- Restoration of energy, sleep, and peace

Spiritual Growth & Intimacy with God

- Hunger for God's Word
- Sensitivity to the Holy Spirit
- Deeper prayer life
- Greater revelation of God's presence

Purpose & Direction

- Clarity in calling or decisions
- Confidence in life direction
- Alignment with God's will
- Open doors and divine appointments

Family & Relationships

- Peace in the home
- Healing in marriages
- Unity among loved ones
- Salvation of family members
- Restoration of broken relationships

Forgiveness & Freedom

- Release from past wounds
- Strength to forgive
- Freedom from shame and guilt
- Breakthrough from spiritual strongholds

Protection & Spiritual Warfare

- Discernment against attacks
- Strength in temptation
- Victory over fear, oppression, and confusion
- Covering over loved ones and homes

Peace, Rest & Joy

- Freedom from stress and unrest
- Deeper emotional rest and contentment

- Lasting joy in all circumstances
- Refreshing in dry seasons

Hope & Future Promise

- Encouragement during delay or waiting
- Renewed vision for what's ahead
- Confidence in God's timing
- Faith for the impossible

Obedience & Discipline

- Strength to follow God's instructions, even when it's hard
- Consistency in spiritual habits (prayer, fasting, reading Scripture)
- Willingness to surrender control and yield to His will
- Endurance to do what's right over what's easy

Wisdom & Discernment

- Clarity in complex decisions
- Discernment between truth and deception
- Sensitivity to the Holy Spirit's leading
- Insight into people, opportunities, and spiritual matters

Calling & Ministry

- Recognition and release of spiritual gifts
- Fruitfulness in serving others
- Boldness in sharing faith
- Open doors to use your life for God's glory

Unity in the Body of Christ

- Healing of division and offenses in the church
- Humility and honor between believers
- Strengthening of spiritual leaders
- A spirit of love, unity, and mission across the global Church

---

Identity & Worth in Christ

- Confidence in who God says I am
- Healing from insecurity, comparison, or rejection
- Living from a place of belovedness, not performance
- Rootedness in grace, not striving

Patience & Perseverance

- Endurance through trials and long waiting seasons
- Joy in the process of becoming
- Strength to continue when progress feels slow
- Trust in God's perfect timing

Creative Expression & Kingdom Innovation

- Using creativity for God's glory
- Boldness to build, write, design, or lead new things
- Fresh vision and divine inspiration
- Wisdom to steward original ideas and initiatives

Time & Priorities

- Discernment in daily decisions and commitments
- Freedom from distraction, overload, and burnout
- Grace to say no and courage to say yes
- Alignment of time and schedule with God's purpose

Emotional Healing & Wholeness

- Healing from emotional wounds and trauma
- Freedom from anxiety, fear, and emotional triggers
- Restoration of peace and inner stability
- Wholeness in identity, relationships, and thought patterns

Justice, Mercy & the Marginalized

- Compassion for the poor, vulnerable, and oppressed
- Boldness to speak up and stand for truth

- Wisdom to act with love, humility, and courage
- Intercession for the hurting and advocacy for change

Faith for Generations to Come

- Prayers and blessings for children and descendants
- Vision for a legacy that honors God
- Spiritual covering over future generations
- Hope for what God will do beyond this lifetime

Dare to Pray Boldly

Faith & Confidence

Scripture Meditation

"Now to Him who is able to do immeasurably more than all we ask or imagine, according to His power that is at work within us..."
– Ephesians 3:20 (NIV)

Reflection: Ask Big, Expect Bigger

God is not intimidated by big prayers, because he is honored by them.
When you ask with boldness, you are not demanding from God, you are agreeing with His nature.
He is able. He is willing. He is faithful.

Your bold prayers create space for God to move in ways that exceed your understanding, and Glorify Him.
So lift your expectations. Ask in faith.
Don't pray like He's distant. Pray like He's listening because He is.

A Bold Prayer of Faith and Confidence

Father God, I come before You not in fear or hesitation, but in the boldness Jesus purchased for me with His blood.
You are the God who parted seas, silenced storms, raised the dead, and still speaks today.
Nothing is too hard for You, and no promise of Yours ever fails.

Today, I ask boldly not because I deserve it, but because You invite me to ask as a child who belongs.
I ask for breakthrough where there has been delay.
I ask for healing where there has been pain.
I ask for open doors where there have been barriers.
I ask for wisdom where I've been unsure, and peace where I've been anxious.

I declare that You are able, You are willing, and You are already at work.
Strengthen my faith. Silence my doubts. Align my heart with Yours.

I believe that You respond to bold faith, and I choose to pray like I believe You are who You say You are.

Let my life become evidence of Your power, Your kindness, and Your faithfulness. Let Your name be glorified.

In the mighty name of Jesus, Amen.

Declaration of Faith and Truth

I am filled with bold faith, rooted in God's promises. I walk with courage, pray with confidence, and refuse to live in fear or double-mindedness.

Faith in Action

Where am I struggling to fully trust God right now? What would it look like to pray, speak, and act with bold confidence in His promises even before I see the outcome?

Faith in Action Response

_____
_____
_____
_____
_____
_____
_____
_____
_____
_____
_____
_____
_____
_____
_____
_____
_____

Act of Gratitude

Write down one thing you're grateful for today that connects with the focus of your prayer.

_____
_____
_____
_____

Things to Remember

_____
_____
_____
_____
_____
_____
_____

Provision and Financial Breakthrough

Scripture Meditation

"And my God will meet all your needs according to the riches of his glory in Christ Jesus."
— Philippians 4:19 (NIV)

Reflection: God Provides from His Riches, Not My Resources

Provision doesn't begin with what I see nor what I think because it begins with who God is.
He is not limited by the economy, my salary, my boss, or what I think is possible.
His supply comes from the riches of His glory, and His generosity flows from His heart as a Father.
He knows every need before I speak it, and He delights in providing for His children. He is interested in, not just enough to survive, but enough to bless others through me.
Provision is more than money. It includes wisdom, opportunities, strength, favor, healing, and open doors.
God provides completely and precisely at the right time, in the right way, and always for my good and His glory.

Bold Prayer for Provision and Financial Breakthrough

Heavenly Father, You are Jehovah Jireh, the God who sees and provides.
I stand before You today not with fear, but with faith.
You own the cattle on a thousand hills, and there is no lack in Your kingdom.
You are not limited by my bank account, the economy, or human systems. You are the Source of all provision.

In the name of Jesus, I ask boldly: Release provision from the north, south, east, and west. Open doors that no one can shut. Send divine opportunities, strategic relationships, and fresh streams of income.
Give me wisdom to manage what You provide and the courage to walk through every door You open.

Break every chain of debt, poverty, fear, and financial limitation. Destroy the lies that say "not enough" and replace them with truth. That truth is, You are more than enough. Let favor go before me, and let abundance follow me, so I may be a blessing to others.

I call forth breakthrough in my finances not for selfish gain, but so that I may glorify You, care for my family, advance Your kingdom, and live in the freedom You designed for me.

I trust You completely. I stand on Your promise in Philippians 4:19 which says *"My God will meet all your needs according to the riches of his glory in Christ Jesus."*

Let it be so, according to Your Word. In Jesus' mighty name, Amen.

Declaration of Faith and Truth

God is my provider. I walk in wisdom and favor. Lack has no place in my life. I receive divine supply and steward every resource with excellence.

Faith in Action

Where in my life do I need God to provide right now?

Is it financially, materially, or through open doors?
What step of faith or obedience can I take today to show that I trust Him as my Provider?

Faith in Action Response

_____
_____
_____
_____
_____
_____
_____
_____
_____
_____
_____
_____
_____
_____

Act of Gratitude

Write down one thing you're grateful for today that connects with the focus of your prayer.

_____
_____
_____
_____

Things to Remember

_____
_____
_____
_____
_____
_____
_____
_____

Healing and Restoration

Scripture Meditation

"Lord my God, I called to you for help, and you healed me."
– Psalm 30:2 (NIV)

Reflection: Healing Begins With a Call

Healing doesn't begin with strength; it begins with surrender. God is not distant or indifferent to your pain. When you call on Him, He listens with compassion and acts with power. Your healing may be instant or may unfold over time, but His heart is always to restore.
Call on Him boldly. Trust Him deeply.
Healing flows where faith and surrender meet.

Bold Prayer for Healing and Restoration

Father God, You are Jehovah Rapha the Lord who heals and nothing is too difficult for You. I come to You in faith, declaring that healing is not just possible, it is part of the promise purchased by the blood of Jesus.

Your Word says in Isaiah 53:5 that *"by His wounds we are healed."* I stand on that truth today.

In the name of Jesus, I speak healing over my body, mind, heart, and soul. I command sickness, pain, disease, and disorder to leave. They have no authority here.
I break every assignment of infirmity, trauma, or generational affliction. Every diagnosis must bow to the name of Jesus. Every system in my body must come into divine alignment with heaven's design.

Restore what has been broken, Lord. Heal not only the physical, but the emotional wounds and places of deep weariness. Restore my joy, my peace, my strength, and my hope. Revive what has been dormant. Renew what has been drained. Make me whole, completely, fully, powerfully, for Your glory.

Let my healing become a testimony. Use it to strengthen the faith of others and remind the world that You are still the God who heals. I will not be moved by what I feel or see. I stand on what You have spoken.

I trust You, God. I receive Your healing, I walk in Your restoration, and I praise You for the victory that is already mine through Christ. In Jesus' mighty name, Amen.

Declaration of Faith and Truth

My body, mind, and spirit are being restored. I receive healing, peace, and strength from the Lord. I am whole and full of life.

Faith in Action

What area of my life in areas of physical, emotional, or spiritual, do I need God to heal or restore?
What truth from Scripture can I speak over that area to replace fear, pain, or disappointment with hope?

Faith in Action Response

_____
_____
_____
_____
_____
_____
_____
_____
_____
_____
_____

Act of Gratitude

Write down one thing you're grateful for today that connects with the focus of your prayer.

_____
_____
_____
_____

Things to Remember

_____
_____
_____
_____
_____
_____
_____
_____

Spiritual Growth & Intimacy with God

Scripture Meditation

"You will seek me and find me when you seek me with all your heart."
– Jeremiah 29:13 (NIV)

Reflection: Intimacy Begins with Desire

God does not hide from those who truly seek Him.
He is not far off. He is near, ready to meet with the one who comes with a whole heart.
Spiritual growth doesn't come from effort alone, but from intimacy with the One who transforms us.
The more you seek Him, the more He reveals Himself, and in His presence, you become more like Him.

Bold Prayer for Spiritual Growth & Intimacy with God

Father, I don't want a surface-level faith or a distant relationship with You.
I want to truly know You more deeply than ever before.
Draw me into the secret place where Your presence is real, Your voice is clear, and my heart becomes fully alive in You.

Remove every barrier that has kept me from intimacy with You.
Break through the distractions, the doubts, the routines, and the noise.
Let my hunger for You be greater than my comfort.
Let my desire for Your presence outweigh my desire for anything else in this world.

I ask boldly for spiritual growth. Grow me in wisdom, in holiness, in discernment, in love, and in unshakable faith.
Let the roots of my spirit go deep, so that when storms come, I will not be moved.
Fill me with Your Spirit. Teach me to hear Your voice, walk in Your truth, and live in constant awareness of You.

I want to walk closely with You every day.
Let Your Word come alive in me. Let prayer become my delight. Let my life be marked by Your presence and transformed by Your glory.

I seek You with all my heart, and I believe You will meet me. I believe You are drawing me near and I respond with a bold yes. Lord, increase my hunger to know You more. I choose to seek You with all my heart. In Jesus' name, Amen.

Declaration of Faith and Truth

I hunger for God and draw near daily. I grow in His Word, listen to His Spirit, and experience His nearness in every moment.

Faith in Action

What is one way I can intentionally create space to be with God this week?
What distractions or habits might I need to release so I can grow closer to Him?

Faith in Action Response

_____
_____
_____
_____
_____
_____
_____
_____
_____
_____

Act of Gratitude

Write down one thing you're grateful for today that connects with the focus of your prayer.

_____
_____
_____
_____

Things to Remember

_____
_____
_____
_____
_____
_____
_____
_____

Purpose & Direction

Scripture Meditation

"The Lord will guide you always; he will satisfy your needs in a sun-scorched land and will strengthen your frame.
You will be like a well-watered garden, like a spring whose waters never fail."
— Isaiah 58:11 (NIV)

Reflection: Direction Is a Promise, Not a Mystery

God is not trying to hide His purpose from you. He promises to guide you.
Even in dry seasons or uncertain moments, He is working behind the scenes, leading you step by step.
You don't have to have the full map to follow His voice.
His direction comes to the heart that is surrendered and willing.
As you trust Him, He will make the path clear and strengthen you to walk it well.

Bold Prayer for Purpose & Direction

Father God, You created me on purpose and for a purpose.
I refuse to wander aimlessly or live by chance when You've called me to walk in destiny.
You are not a God of confusion, and I know You have a plan for my life. A plan for my life that is good, fruitful, and full of meaning.

Right now, I ask boldly for clarity. Open my eyes to see what You've prepared for me. Open my ears to hear Your instruction, and open my heart to trust Your timing.
Silence every voice that brings doubt, distraction, or delay and amplify the voice of Your Spirit in my life.

I surrender my own plans, and I ask for Your direction. Where You lead, I will follow.
If You say go, I'll move. If You say wait, I'll trust. If You say no, I'll let go. Order my steps according to Your Word, and align my heart with Your will.

Let my life count for something eternal.
Show me how to use my gifts, my time, and my voice for Your kingdom. Use my journey to impact others, glorify Your name, and bring heaven's purpose to earth through me.

I believe You are guiding me even when I can't see every step. I believe You are faithful to finish what You've started. So I move forward in faith and not in fear because You go before me. God, I trust You to lead me. I may not see the full picture, but I believe You are ordering every step."

In Jesus' mighty name, Amen.

Declaration of Faith and Truth

God orders my steps. I am clear, confident, and aligned with His purpose. Doors open, wisdom flows, and I walk in divine direction.

Faith in Action

What step of obedience can I take today even if it's small, to align with His purpose for me?

Faith in Action Response

Act of Gratitude

Write down one thing you're grateful for today that connects with the focus of your prayer.

_____
_____
_____
_____

Things to Remember

_____
_____
_____
_____
_____
_____
_____
_____

Family & Relationships

Scripture Meditation

"But as for me and my household, we will serve the Lord."
– Joshua 24:15 (NIV)

Reflection: God Can Heal Any Home

God's desire is to bless individuals and to bless households. Even when things look broken or strained, He is able to restore what was lost, soften hearts, and rewrite family stories.

Healing begins with surrender. As you trust Him with your relationships, He will begin working in ways you can't always see but can always believe.

No relationship is too far gone. No heart is too hard.

When God is at the center, even the most fragile bond can be rebuilt with strength and grace.

Bold Prayer for Family & Relationships

Father, You are the God who created family, who places the lonely in families, and who binds hearts together in love.
I come to You today with boldness, asking for Your power to move through every relationship in my life, especially those closest to me. Where there has been division, bring unity. Where there has been pain, bring healing. Where there has been silence, bring understanding. Where there has been dysfunction, bring restoration and peace.

Cover my family with Your protection. Let love be the atmosphere in our home. Let kindness and forgiveness run deeper than pride or hurt. I bind the enemy's attempts to sow strife, confusion, or bitterness, and I declare that my household belongs to You.

Strengthen marriages. Restore the hearts of parents and children to one another.
Bring salvation to those who are far from You. Break generational cycles that do not reflect Your truth, and plant seeds of legacy that will bear fruit for generations.

Teach me how to love like You love. Give me patience, wisdom, humility, and courage to serve, speak life, and stand firm in truth. Let my relationships reflect the beauty and power of the gospel.

You are a God of reconciliation. You are the God who turns hearts of stone into hearts of flesh. So I trust You for what I see now, and for the healing, unity, and blessing You are already bringing, which I cannot see now. In the name of Jesus, Amen.

Declaration of Faith and Truth

My home is filled with peace. God is restoring every relationship. Love leads, healing flows, and salvation belongs to my household.

Faith in Action

Who is one person I need to forgive, bless, or pray for today? What step of love or grace can I take toward them?

Faith in Action Response

_____
_____
_____
_____
_____
_____
_____
_____
_____
_____
_____
_____

Act of Gratitude

Write down one thing you're grateful for today that connects with the focus of your prayer.

_____
_____
_____
_____

Things to Remember

_____
_____
_____
_____
_____
_____
_____
_____
_____

Forgiveness & Freedom

Scripture Meditation

"So if the Son sets you free, you will be free indeed."
— John 8:36 (NIV)

Reflection: Forgiveness Breaks Chains, Freedom Follows

True freedom begins with forgiveness, receiving it from God and releasing it toward others.
Unforgiveness keeps you tied to pain that Jesus already died to heal.
The enemy thrives in bitterness and shame, but Jesus brings healing, wholeness, and liberty.
When you forgive, you're not excusing the wrong; you're cutting the cord that keeps you bound to it.
When you believe in God's forgiveness over your past, you step into the fullness of who He's called you to be.
Freedom isn't just possible, it's already been purchased.

Bold Prayer for Forgiveness & Freedom

Father God,
I thank You that through the blood of Jesus, I am not bound to my past. I am set free.
You are the God who forgives sin, breaks chains, and restores what was lost.
I come to You boldly today, not to hide, but to be healed.
I confess the places in my heart that have held bitterness, shame, guilt, or regret and I lay them down at Your feet.

Right now, I receive Your forgiveness.
Wash me clean. Silence the voice of the accuser.
I refuse to live under condemnation when You have called me forgiven, restored, and made new.
Let the weight of guilt be lifted.
Let the lies of shame be broken.
Let the cross speak louder than my failures.

Lord, I choose to forgive.
I release those who have hurt me, not because they deserve it, but because I refuse to stay chained to the pain.
I forgive by faith, and I ask You to help me walk in that freedom daily. Heal the wounds I still feel.
Uproot the bitterness trying to take root.
Fill those places with Your love, peace, and healing power.

I declare that I am no longer a prisoner to my past. I am a child of God, free and fully accepted in Christ.
Let freedom ring in my mind, in my emotions, in my relationships, and in every corner of my soul. I will walk in freedom because I belong to You. In Jesus' name, Amen.

Declaration of Faith and Truth

I am no longer bound by shame or pain. I forgive freely, live freely, and walk in the victory of Christ's freedom.

Faith in Action

What burden, regret, or hurt do I need to release today? What truth from God's Word can I hold onto in its place?

Faith in Action Response

_____
_____
_____
_____
_____
_____
_____
_____
_____
_____
_____

Act of Gratitude

Write down one thing you're grateful for today that connects with the focus of your prayer.

_____
_____
_____
_____

Things to Remember

_____
_____
_____
_____
_____
_____
_____
_____

Protection & Spiritual Warfare

Scripture Meditation

"The Lord will fight for you; you need only to be still."
– Exodus 14:14 (NIV)

Reflection: You Don't Fight Alone

Regarding spiritual warfare do not strive in your own strength. Stand in the victory. Jesus already won.
God doesn't ask you to be powerful on your own. He equips you, covers you, and fights for you.
The enemy's goal is intimidation, distraction, and fear but God gives you clarity, authority, and peace.
When you remain rooted in His truth and presence, you stand in territory the enemy cannot overtake.
So don't back down. Don't bow to fear.
Stand still, stand firm, and let God show Himself strong on your behalf.

Bold Prayer for Protection & Spiritual Warfare

Almighty God,
I thank You that I am fighting from victory.
Through the blood of Jesus and the power of His name, I take my stand today against every scheme of the enemy.
No weapon formed against me will prosper, and every tongue that rises against me will be silenced.

I put on the full armor of God:
The belt of truth to guard my mind from lies,
The breastplate of righteousness to protect my heart,
The shoes of peace to keep me grounded in Your Word,
The shield of faith to extinguish every fiery dart,
The helmet of salvation to cover my thoughts,
And the sword of the Spirit which is Your Word to strike down every deception.

Lord, I declare that I belong to You.
I reject every fear, lie, and accusation that has tried to attach itself to me. I speak the name of Jesus over my home, my family, my thoughts, my body, and every place I walk.
No darkness has power here.
Every stronghold must break.
Every spirit of confusion, oppression, heaviness, or fear must go now, in the mighty name of Jesus.

Fill me with boldness.
Help me discern quickly and resist firmly.
Let me stand my ground in prayer and walk daily in Your authority, knowing that the battle is Yours and You have already won it. In the omnipotent and undefeated name of Jesus, Amen.

Declaration of Faith and Truth

I am protected, discerning, and secure. I walk in authority, resist the enemy, and stand strong in God's power and truth.

Faith in Action

Where do I sense spiritual pressure or resistance in my life right now? What truth from God's Word can I stand on to respond in faith and authority?

Faith in Action Response

_____
_____
_____
_____
_____
_____
_____
_____
_____
_____
_____

Act of Gratitude

Write down one thing you're grateful for today that connects with the focus of your prayer.

_____
_____
_____
_____

Things to Remember

_____
_____
_____
_____
_____
_____
_____
_____

Peace, Rest & Joy

Scripture Meditation

"You make known to me the path of life; you will fill me with joy in your presence, with eternal pleasures at your right hand."
– Psalm 16:11 (NIV)

Reflection: Joy and Rest Are Found in His Presence

True peace flows from being with the One who holds everything in His hands.
Rest in your worship.
Don't let your joy be based on circumstances. Joy is the strength that comes from knowing you're never alone.
When you slow down and turn your heart toward God, He fills the empty places with peace, refreshes your spirit with rest, and restores your joy like a wellspring that never runs dry.

Bold Prayer for Peace, Rest & Joy

Father God,
You are the God of peace, the Giver of true rest, and the source of everlasting joy.
I refuse to live weighed down by stress, fear, or unrest because You have promised peace that surpasses understanding.
Today, I boldly lay down every burden, every anxious thought, and every heavy emotion. I cast them at Your feet, and I receive Your supernatural peace in their place.

Silence every storm in my mind.
Calm the noise that keeps me from hearing Your voice.
I choose to rest, not because everything is perfect, but because You are still on the throne and You are with me.

I speak rest over my body, soul, and spirit.
I declare that my worth is not in what I produce, but in who I belong to. I reject every lie that tells me I must strive, perform, or prove myself. Your presence is my refuge. In You, I find renewal.

Father, I ask for joy, real joy; not circumstantial happiness, but deep, sustaining joy rooted in who You are.
Let joy bubble up from the inside.
Let laughter return to my home.
Let the oil of gladness replace every spirit of heaviness.
I choose to rejoice in my Savior, and not worry about my situation.

I thank You, Lord, for being my peace, my rest, and my joy now and always in the powerful name of Jesus, Amen.

Declaration of Faith and Truth

I live from a place of deep peace and overflowing joy. My soul is at rest, my heart is light, and my joy is full.

Faith in Action

What is stealing my peace right now, and what would it look like to surrender that burden fully to God?
Where can I intentionally create space for rest this week and what brings me joy that reconnects me to His presence?

Faith in Action Response

_____
_____
_____
_____
_____
_____
_____
_____
_____
_____
_____

Act of Gratitude

Write down one thing you're grateful for today that connects with the focus of your prayer.

_____
_____
_____
_____

Things to Remember

_____
_____
_____
_____
_____
_____
_____
_____

Hope & Future Promise

Scripture Meditation

"'For I know the plans I have for you,' declares the Lord, 'plans to prosper you and not to harm you, plans to give you a hope and a future.'"
– Jeremiah 29:11 (NIV)

Reflection: Hope Is Rooted in God's Faithfulness, Not Life's Certainty

Hope is confident expectation in the One who holds your tomorrow.
Even when the path feels delayed or unclear, God's plans are never lost.
He sees beyond the present and prepares you for what you cannot yet see.
Hope grows when you choose to trust God's timeline over your own and believe that His promises are still unfolding even in the quiet.

Bold Prayer for Hope & Future Promise

Father God,
You are the God of hope, the One who writes my future with wisdom, purpose, and love.
You are not finished with me. Even when I can't see the way forward, I believe Your plans for me are good.
I reject despair. I refuse to be led by fear, delay, or discouragement.
Today, I anchor my hope in You, not in outcomes, timelines, or circumstances, but in Your unchanging character.

Breathe fresh vision into my soul.
Restore what disappointment tried to steal.
Awaken the dreams You placed within me and give me the strength to believe again.
I declare that my future is in Your hands, and nothing the enemy has done can cancel what You have promised.

Open doors that no one can shut.
Let hope rise like the morning sun.
Even in waiting, I will trust. Even in silence, I will worship.
Even in uncertainty, I will walk by faith.

You are the Author of my story. You are the Redeemer of my past, the strength in my present, and the architect of my tomorrow. I believe You are working behind the scenes, aligning every detail for Your glory and my good.

I will not give up. I will not grow bitter.
I will move forward with faith, courage, and expectation because You, Lord, are faithful to the end. In the name of Jesus, Amen.

Declaration of Faith and Truth

I will not lose heart. My future is in God's hands. I wait with faith, dream with hope, and expect the impossible.

Faith in Action

What promise from God do I need to hold onto right now? How can I choose hope over discouragement today?

Faith in Action Response

_____
_____
_____
_____
_____
_____
_____
_____
_____
_____
_____
_____

Act of Gratitude

Write down one thing you're grateful for today that connects with the focus of your prayer.

_____
_____
_____
_____

Things to Remember

_____
_____
_____
_____
_____
_____
_____
_____

Obedience & Discipline

Scripture Meditation

"If you love me, keep my commands."
— John 14:15 (NIV)

Reflection: Obedience Is the Fruit of Love, Not Obligation

God isn't looking for perfectio; He's looking for a heart that says yes.
Obedience isn't just about rules; it's the overflow of love and trust.
Discipline grows when you love God more than your comfort and when you value His Word above your own feelings.
Each act of obedience shapes you into who you're becoming, a disciple who doesn't just hear the truth, but lives it.
Faithful obedience, day by day, is what turns belief into breakthrough.

Bold Prayer for Obedience & Discipline

Lord God,
You are worthy of more than my intentions. You are worthy of my obedience. Today, I refuse to live by feelings, excuses, or half-hearted devotion.
I want to be a disciple, not just in name but in action fully surrendered, fully engaged, fully Yours.

Give me the strength to obey You when it's difficult, inconvenient, or unclear.
Train my heart to say "yes" quickly when You speak.
Form in me the discipline to follow through, to show up in prayer, to stay in Your Word, and to live with purpose even when no one sees.

Break off laziness, distraction, and spiritual apathy.
Tear down every pattern of delay, compromise, and self-sabotage.
Build in me a lifestyle of discipline that honors You driven by love and passion for Your presence.

Lord, I don't want a life that merely hears truth. I want a life that lives it. Shape my habits. Align my time with Your priorities. Teach me to obey even when I don't understand, and to keep walking even when I don't feel like it.

Let me be found faithful.
Let my life be marked by consistency, humility, and strength.
Empower me, Holy Spirit, to run this race with endurance one obedient step at a time.

In the mighty name of Jesus, Amen.

Declaration of Faith and Truth

I obey with joy and discipline my life around God's will. I endure when it's hard and grow stronger in spiritual habits.

Faith in Action

Where am I hesitating to obey God fully? What one small, obedient step can I take today to align my life with His will?

Faith in Action Response

_____
_____
_____
_____
_____
_____
_____
_____
_____
_____
_____
_____

Act of Gratitude

Write down one thing you're grateful for today that connects with the focus of your prayer.

_____
_____
_____
_____

Things to Remember

_____
_____
_____
_____
_____
_____
_____
_____

Wisdom & Discernment

Scripture Meditation

"If any of you lacks wisdom, you should ask God, who gives generously to all without finding fault, and it will be given to you."
– James 1:5 (NIV)

Reflection: Wisdom Is a Promise, Not a Privilege

God never intended for you to navigate life by guessing.
He invites you to ask, and He promises to answer.
Wisdom isn't reserved for the elite or the experienced. It's available to anyone willing to pause, ask, and listen.
When you pursue wisdom in prayer and the Word, your decisions gain clarity, your spirit gains peace, and your life gains direction.
Discernment helps you see beyond what's visible and choose what aligns with God's heart even when it isn't the obvious path.

Bold Prayer for Wisdom & Discernment

Lord of all wisdom,
You are not the author of confusion. You are the Giver of clarity, insight, and truth.
Right now, I ask boldly for what You promised to give generously: wisdom from above.
Not the wisdom of this world, but wisdom that comes from Your Spirit, pure, peace-loving, full of mercy, and unwavering in truth.

I ask You to sharpen my discernment. Help me see what others may not see. Expose deception quickly. Make my spirit sensitive to Your warnings, Your nudges, and Your guidance. When I face a crossroads, let Your voice rise above every other voice. Teach me to think with clarity, speak with conviction, and act with precision.

Break every pattern of confusion and double-mindedness. Silence the noise of fear, flesh, and false counsel.
Guard me from distractions disguised as opportunity.
Let my decisions align with Your will, and let Your peace confirm every step.

Fill me with the mind of Christ. Let Your Word dwell richly in me, shaping how I think, how I lead, and how I love.
Let the fear of the Lord not the opinions of people but let it be the foundation of my choices.

You are the Wonderful Counselor, the Eternal Rock of Wisdom. Lead me in truth. Keep me in truth.
And use my life to reflect the beauty and strength of a Spirit-led mind. In Jesus' name, Amen.

Declaration of Faith and Truth

I have divine clarity. I discern truth from lies and walk wisely in every decision. God's insight leads me daily.

Faith in Action

Where do I need God's wisdom right now? What distractions do I need to quiet so I can discern His voice clearly?

Faith in Action Response

_____
_____
_____
_____
_____
_____
_____
_____
_____
_____
_____

Act of Gratitude

Write down one thing you're grateful for today that connects with the focus of your prayer.

_____
_____
_____
_____

Things to Remember

_____
_____
_____
_____
_____
_____
_____
_____

Calling & Ministry

Scripture Meditation

"For we are God's handiwork, created in Christ Jesus to do good works, which God prepared in advance for us to do."
— Ephesians 2:10 (NIV)

Reflection: You Were Made for This

Your calling is divine.
Before you were born, God handcrafted you with gifts, experiences, and passions that align with a specific purpose. You don't have to strive to find it because you were made for it. The more you surrender, the clearer the path becomes. Your ministry may not look like anyone else's, and that's exactly the point.
You are uniquely positioned to reflect God's glory and reach people no one else can.

Bold Prayer for Calling & Ministry

Father God,
You have called me by name, and I believe You have marked my life with purpose. Before I was born, You set me apart not just to believe, but to build, serve, lead, and carry Your presence into the world. I will no longer shrink back. I will not delay. I say yes to the calling You've placed on my life.

Ignite the gifts You've deposited within me.
Uncover what has been hidden. Awaken what has been dormant. Break off fear, comparison, and the lies that have kept me silent or sidelined.
I am not here to live small I am here to walk boldly in the ministry You've prepared for me.

Whether the assignment is in the spotlight or in secret, I will serve with faithfulness and fire.
Show me where to go, who to reach, and what to release.
Open the doors You've ordained, and close the ones that would distract or derail me.
Surround me with people who sharpen my calling and stir my spirit.

Let my ministry be marked by Your presence, Your power, and Your love. Use my voice to speak life. Use my hands to serve others. Use my life to glorify You.

I don't want comfort, I want calling.
I don't want applause, I want anointing.
I don't want to be busy, I want to be effective.

So I yield fully. I move forward boldly.
Here I am, Lord, send me. In Jesus' name, Amen.

Declaration of Faith and Truth

I am called, equipped, and sent. My gifts bear fruit, my service honors God, and my life is a light to others.

Faith in Action

What has God placed in my hands right now that He may be calling me to use for His glory? What step of obedience can I take to walk in that calling with confidence?

Faith in Action Response

_____
_____
_____
_____
_____
_____
_____
_____
_____
_____
_____

Act of Gratitude

Write down one thing you're grateful for today that connects with the focus of your prayer.

_____
_____
_____
_____

Things to Remember

_____
_____
_____
_____
_____
_____
_____

Unity in the Body of Christ

Scripture Meditation

"Make every effort to keep the unity of the Spirit through the bond of peace. There is one body and one Spirit, just as you were called to one hope when you were called."
– Ephesians 4:3–4 (NIV)

Reflection: Unity Is a Spiritual Priority, Not an Optional Ideal

Unity is the supernatural oneness that believers share through faith in Jesus Christ, rooted in the truth of God's Word, empowered by the Holy Spirit, and expressed in love, humility, and mutual purpose. Unity is not uniformity but a deep spiritual connection that flows from shared identity in Christ.

The Body of Christ is most powerful when it is most united. The enemy works through division, but God moves through agreement.
When believers choose love over offense, truth over ego, and peace over personal preference, the Church becomes unstoppable.
Unity is pursued by choice, and it begins with each of us.

Bold Prayer for Unity in the Body of Christ

Father,
You are not the God of division. You are the God of unity, harmony, and oneness. Your Son prayed that we would be one, just as You and He are one. So today, I come boldly before You, asking for a move of unity across Your people.

Tear down every wall of offense, pride, competition, and misunderstanding. Break the strongholds of comparison, control, and spiritual pride.
Heal the wounds that have kept Your Body fractured.
Make us one Church, with one heart, one mission, and one Spirit that is the Spirit of truth and love.

Unite leaders, churches, generations, and races under the lordship of Jesus Christ.
Let love be louder than doctrine.
Let humility be greater than position.
Let the power of the cross be the foundation of our relationships.

Use us, together, to bring healing to our communities and light to the world.
Help me do my part which is to forgive quickly, honor freely, serve joyfully, and speak life consistently.
Let my words and actions build unity, not division.

May the world know we belong to You by the way we love one another. Bind us together in truth. Ignite us together in purpose.
Let the Church rise in unity and power as a reflection of heaven on earth. In Jesus' name, Amen.

Declaration of Faith and Truth

I am a bridge of unity and healing in the body of Christ. I honor others, support leaders, and walk in love and humility.

Faith in Action

Where do I need to release offense, extend forgiveness, or build a bridge within the Body of Christ? What can I do to reflect Christ's love to those who are different from me?

Faith in Action Response

Act of Gratitude

Write down one thing you're grateful for today that connects with the focus of your prayer.

_____
_____
_____
_____

Things to Remember

_____
_____
_____
_____
_____
_____
_____
_____

Identity & Worth in Christ

Scripture Meditation

"See what great love the Father has lavished on us, that we should be called children of God! And that is what we are!"
–1 John 3:1 (NIV)

"For we are God's masterpiece. He has created us anew in Christ Jesus, so we can do the good things he planned for us long ago."
–Ephesians 2:10 (NLT)

Reflection

There is a fierce battle over identity in the heart of every believer. The world, the enemy, and even past wounds can distort how we see ourselves. But God speaks a better word. He calls you His child, His masterpiece, His chosen one. Your worth is not earned. It was declared at the cross and sealed by His Spirit.

When we live from a place of identity in Christ, we stop striving for approval and start living in freedom. We serve with confidence, not insecurity. We walk in love, not fear. We rest in grace, not perfectionism. God does not measure your value by what you produce, how others see you, or even by how you feel about yourself. He calls you beloved. This is the starting place for everything else.

Bold Prayer for Identity & Worth in Christ

Father, Thank You for creating me with intention, shaping me with love, and calling me with purpose. Before I took my first breath, You already had a plan for my life.

You chose me. You named me. You saw value in me that this world could never define or diminish. Forgive me for listening to every voice but Yours including the voices of insecurity, rejection, comparison, and shame. Forgive me for believing lies that say I'm too much, not enough, or unworthy of love.

Today, I renounce every false label, every wound of the past, and every identity I've worn that You never gave me. I declare that I am who You say I am, Chosen, beloved, redeemed, holy, set apart, and deeply known. Heal the places in me that have been shaped by rejection instead of truth. Tear down every stronghold of self-doubt, self-hate, or self-promotion. Silence the inner critic. Cancel the echo of old wounds. Let the voice of my Father thunder louder than the opinions of men.

I choose to live from the confidence of being Yours and not for approval, but from it. Let my worth be rooted in the cross, not in performance. Let my identity be unshakable, even when circumstances shift. I will no longer chase the applause of people. I will live for the affirmation that comes from heaven. You have called me by name and written my identity in Your book. I receive it. I believe it. And I will walk in it with boldness and peace. I am not what I've done, what I've lost, or what others have said. I am Your child, called, chosen, and covered. In the mighty name of Jesus, Amen.

Declaration of Faith and Truth

"I am a child of God, loved, chosen, and made new. My value is not based on what I do but on whose I am. I am free from shame, rooted in grace, and secure in Christ."

Faith in Action

What lies have shaped how you view yourself, and how is God rewriting those lies with truth? Write a statement of identity grounded in Scripture that you want to live from today.

Faith in Action Response

Act of Gratitude

Write down one thing you're grateful for today that connects with the focus of your prayer.

_____
_____
_____
_____

Things to Remember

_____
_____
_____
_____
_____
_____
_____
_____

Patience & Perseverance

Scripture Meditation

"Let perseverance finish its work so that you may be mature and complete, not lacking anything."
–James 1:4 (NIV)

"But if we hope for what we do not yet have, we wait for it patiently."
–Romans 8:25 (NIV)

Reflection

There are seasons when God seems silent, doors stay closed, and progress feels painfully slow. It's in those moments that patience becomes more than a virtue. It becomes a spiritual weapon. Waiting with faith is not passive. It is a declaration that God is still at work even when we cannot see it.

Perseverance grows when we hold onto God's promises and keep walking forward, even when the outcome is unclear. These moments stretch us, but they also shape us. They expose false timelines, test our motivations, and deepen our dependence on God.

God is never late. He is always working beneath the surface, preparing both the blessing and the believer. When we endure with hope, we are strengthened, refined, and made ready for what's next.

Bold Prayer for Patience & Perserverance

Lord of perfect timing, You are never late, never rushed, and never uncertain. You are the Author of my story, the Keeper of my days, and the One who knows the end from the beginning. So today, I surrender the pace of my life to You.

Teach me how to wait faithfully. When my heart grows restless, anchor me in Your promises. When impatience rises, remind me that Your delays are often divine preparations.

I confess that I've grown weary in the waiting.
I've doubted Your timing and questioned Your silence.
But now I choose trust over torment, surrender over striving. You are working even when I don't see it. You are shaping me even in the stillness.

Let this waiting season refine me, not define me. Build endurance where there was frustration. Build hope where there was delay. Build unshakable faith that clings to You, even when the breakthrough hasn't come.

Open my eyes to the purpose in this pause. Let me grow deeper before I go further. Let me be equipped before I'm elevated. Let my waiting be worship, not worry.

Strengthen my hands for the next season. Steady my heart so I don't move ahead of You. And when I'm tempted to give up, remind me: You are still writing. You are still faithful. And You are never finished with me. I declare that this waiting is not wasted. You are preparing me for what You've already prepared for me. And I will wait with fire in my faith.

In the name of Jesus, my Hope and my Anchor, Amen.

Declaration of Faith and Truth

I am not forgotten. God is working even when I cannot see. God is shaping me through every delay. I choose to wait with faith, walk with endurance, and believe that His timing is perfect and His purpose will prevail. I choose joy in the process.

Faith in Action

Where in your life are you being asked to wait or persevere? How is God inviting you to trust Him more deeply in this area?

Faith in Action Response

_____
_____
_____
_____
_____
_____
_____
_____
_____
_____

Act of Gratitude

Write down one thing you're grateful for today that connects with the focus of your prayer.

_____
_____
_____
_____

Things to Remember

_____
_____
_____
_____
_____
_____
_____
_____

Creative Expression & Kingdom Innovation

Scripture Meditation

"See, I have filled him with the Spirit of God, with wisdom, with understanding, with knowledge and with all kinds of skills—to make artistic designs..."
—Exodus 31:3–4 (NIV)

"Whatever you do, work at it with all your heart, as working for the Lord, not for human masters."
—Colossians 3:23 (NIV)

Reflection

God is the ultimate Creator. He speaks galaxies into existence and breathes life into dust. That same Spirit of creativity lives in you. Whether you express it through art, writing, music, entrepreneurship, problem-solving, or building systems, your creativity carries purpose. It is part of how you reflect the image of God. Creative expression when surrendered to the Holy Spirit, becomes Kingdom innovation, and a way to communicate truth, serve others, challenge norms, and bring beauty into dark places. God delights in breathing on what you dare to offer Him.

This is a call to create, not for applause or perfection, but for glory. You are not disqualified because you are unconventional. Your ideas are not too small. When you yield your creativity to God, He multiplies its reach and makes it holy.

Bold Prayer for Creative Expression & Kingdom Innovation

Father,
You are the Master Creator, the One who spoke galaxies into existence and formed beauty from dust. You made me in Your image, which means You designed me to imagine, build, write, speak, sing, lead, design, and release what reflects Your heart.

Thank You for placing creativity, insight, and vision inside of me. Forgive me for the times I've buried my gifts, silenced my voice, or let fear convince me I'm not enough.
Today, I offer You everything You've placed in my hands, every idea, every dream, every project, every talent, not for my glory, but for Yours.

Breathe on my creativity, Lord. Awaken fresh ideas that solve real problems, reveal Your truth, and carry Your beauty into dark spaces. Let my work be more than skill; let it be Spirit-led. Let it be innovation that reveals the fingerprints of heaven.

Break every chain of comparison, perfectionism, hesitation, and fear of man. Remind me that if You gave it to me, You intend to use it. I will not play small when You've called me to shine boldly for Your kingdom.

Give me supernatural courage to create even when no one is watching, to build even when it's unfamiliar, to speak even when my voice shakes, and to finish what You've started in me.

Let my creativity serve others, heal hearts, and make space for Your presence.
Let every song, sentence, canvas, code, or concept I offer be filled with Your breath and Your brilliance.

Not for applause. Not for platform. But to glorify the One who created all things.

I am not just an artist, thinker, writer, leader, builder but I am a vessel for Kingdom innovation.

So come, Holy Spirit, anoint my mind, awaken my imagination, and flow through my hands.
Let my creative expression carry the weight of heaven, and let it point the world back to You.

In the name of Jesus, the Creator, the Word, the Truth, and the Light, Amen.

Declaration of Faith and Truth

I am created in the image of God and filled with His Spirit. My creativity has purpose. What I build matters. I will not hide my gift. I will use it boldly and trust Him to multiply the impact. God breathes on my ideas and uses them for His glory.

Faith in Action (Journal Prompt)

What creative gift, idea, or project has God placed on your heart that you've delayed or dismissed? What small step can you take today to move forward in faith?

Faith in Action Response

Act of Gratitude

Write down one thing you're grateful for today that connects with the focus of your prayer.

_____
_____
_____
_____

Things to Remember

_____
_____
_____
_____
_____
_____
_____
_____

Time & Priorities

Scripture Meditation

"Be very careful, then, how you live – not as unwise but as wise, making the most of every opportunity, because the days are evil."
–Ephesians 5:15–16 (NIV)

"But seek first His kingdom and His righteousness, and all these things will be given to you as well."
–Matthew 6:33 (NIV)

Reflection

Time is one of the most valuable resources we've been given. Once spent, it cannot be recovered. Yet in the rush of life, our calendars fill, our minds race, and our attention drifts. If we're not intentional, good things can crowd out the most important things.

God invites us to live wisely and purposefully. He does not call us to exhaustion, but to alignment. He knows what truly matters and desires to help us reorder our days around what brings life, not just busyness. When we put Him first, everything else finds its rightful place.

Praying about our time is not just about productivity. It's about stewardship. It's about slowing down long enough to listen, letting go of what doesn't belong, and embracing rhythms that nourish our soul. It's the sacred act of choosing what aligns with God's will and releasing what doesn't.

Bold Prayer for Time & Priorities

Lord of time and eternity,
You hold my days in Your hands, and You've appointed purpose to every moment of my life.
You are not the author of chaos, anxiety, or exhaustion but You are the God of wisdom, order, and peace.

I confess I've filled my life with too much noise, obligations, and too little space for You.
I've chased after things that don't last, and I've often said yes when You were calling me to be still.
But today, I surrender my time back to You.

Teach me to number my days and to honor You with them.
Break every addiction to busyness, every fear of missing out, every identity tied to doing instead of being.
Give me eyes to see what really matters which is what You've actually called me to, and the courage to release everything else.

Interrupt my patterns if You must.
Disrupt my schedule if it keeps me from hearing You.
Let Your Spirit set my pace. I do not want pressure, people, or performance to set my pace.

Give me divine clarity: what to start, what to stop, what to hold, and what to hand off.
Help me choose obedience over obligation. Presence over productivity. Surrender over striving.

Align my priorities with heaven.
Let my calendar reflect Your purpose, not just my ambition.
Let rest be holy. Let work be fruitful. Let every hour be redeemed for Your glory.

Lord, in all of it teach me to sit at Your feet like Mary, and not be anxious like Martha.
Because You are my portion, and nothing matters more than being with You.

I declare that my time belongs to You. My priorities are set by You.
And my life will no longer be driven by the urgent, but by the eternal.

In the powerful name of Jesus,
Amen.

Declaration of Faith and Truth

"My time belongs to God. I will not be ruled by urgency, distraction, or fear of missing out. I choose to live wisely, seek what matters most, and walk in step with God's purpose for my days."

Faith in Action

What activity, habit, or commitment is taking time away from what matters most? What is one adjustment you can make this week to better align your time with God's priorities for your life?

Faith in Action Response

_____
_____
_____
_____
_____
_____
_____
_____
_____
_____
_____

Act of Gratitude

Write down one thing you're grateful for today that connects with the focus of your prayer.

_____
_____
_____
_____

Things to Remember

_____
_____
_____
_____
_____
_____
_____
_____

Emotional Healing & Wholeness

Scripture Meditation

"He heals the brokenhearted and binds up their wounds."
–Psalm 147:3 (NIV)

"The Lord is close to the brokenhearted and saves those who are crushed in spirit."
–Psalm 34:18 (NIV)

Reflection

Some wounds go deeper than the physical. They live in our memories, our patterns, and our inner dialogue. Emotional pain can come from loss, betrayal, rejection, trauma, or disappointment. Left unaddressed, these wounds shape how we see ourselves, how we respond to others, and how we approach God.

But the heart is not beyond healing. God sees every invisible bruise and knows every silent ache. He is interested in more than behavior. He desires wholeness. Wholeness doesn't mean perfection. It means walking in freedom, peace, and stability, even if your story includes pain.

Healing often takes time. It may involve tears, forgiveness, and courageous honesty. But it is worth it. God wants to restore what was broken and redeem what was lost. He is both the healer and the safe place where healing begins.

Bold Prayer for Emotional Healing & Wholeness

Father of mercy and healing,
You see every part of me, the pain I hide, the memories I've buried, the emotions I've suppressed, and the tears I never let fall. You know where the wounds are, even when I've forgotten them. You know what broke me, what scarred me, what silenced me and still, You call me yours.

I no longer want to carry these burdens alone.
So today, I open every locked room in my soul.
Come in, Lord. Come into the grief, the fear, the anger, the shame, and the silent ache I can't put into words.
I invite You into every unresolved place within me to heal it.

Where trauma has taken root, plant peace.
Where anxiety has grown, let faith arise.
Where bitterness has lived, let forgiveness flow.
Where I've lived under labels, lies, or self-hate, replace them with truth that sets me free.

Tear down every false identity, every emotional wall, and every coping mechanism that has kept me from real healing.
I release the pain I've tried to control.
I give You permission to rewrite my story by redeeming it with Your power and love.

Heal me not just emotionally, but spiritually and relationally.
Make me whole in my mind, whole in my heart, whole in my soul.
I want to flourish and to be fully alive in You.

Where there has been a wound, let there now be a testimony.
Where there has been silence, let worship rise.
Where there has been fear, let boldness emerge.
Use even this pain for Your glory, and let healing flow like a river through every part of my life.

You are the God who binds up the brokenhearted, and I am not beyond Your reach.
I receive Your healing now, by faith.
I declare that my emotions will no longer control me but that Your Spirit will.

In the name of Jesus, who came to heal every hurt and restore every soul,
Amen.

Declaration of Faith and Truth

"I am not my pain. I am not my past. I am a child of God, and He is healing every place in me that has been broken. My heart is safe in His hands, and my wholeness is His will."

Faith in Action

What emotions or past experiences still affect you today? How is God inviting you to begin or continue the process of healing?

Faith in Action Response

_____
_____
_____
_____
_____
_____
_____
_____
_____
_____
_____
_____

Act of Gratitude

Write down one thing you're grateful for today that connects with the focus of your prayer.

_____
_____
_____
_____

Things to Remember

_____
_____
_____
_____
_____
_____
_____
_____

Justice, Mercy & the Marginalized

Scripture Meditation

"He has shown you, O mortal, what is good. And what does the Lord require of you? To act justly and to love mercy and to walk humbly with your God."

–Micah 6:8 (NIV)

"Speak up for those who cannot speak for themselves, for the rights of all who are destitute. Speak up and judge fairly; defend the rights of the poor and needy."

–Proverbs 31:8–9 (NIV)

Reflection

God's heart beats with justice, compassion, and mercy. Throughout Scripture, He identifies with the poor, oppressed, outcast, and broken. He commands His people to do the same. The pursuit of justice is deeply spiritual. It reflects His character. When we pray for justice, we align with the work of heaven. When we intercede for the marginalized, we echo the prayers of Jesus, who spent His life lifting the lowly and confronting injustice. Mercy is strength clothed in compassion. Justice is the restoration of dignity and order according to God's design. Whether you are called to advocate, serve, give, or simply begin by seeing people the way God sees them, your prayers are part of how God's justice moves into the world. You may not fix every broken system, but you can reflect His heart in every space you enter.

Bold Prayer for Justice, Mercy & the Marginalized

Father of righteousness and mercy,
You are the Defender of the weak, the Father to the fatherless, the Shelter for the oppressed, and the God who sees. You have always lifted the lowly and torn down the proud. You have always stood with the overlooked and silenced the voice of the oppressor. And today, I align my heart with Yours.

Let holy fire rise within me not just for comfort, but for courage. Open my eyes to what I have ignored. Break my heart for what breaks Yours. Strip away selfishness, apathy, and fear, and clothe me in conviction, compassion, and love that takes action.

Make me a voice that carries Your truth and not mere opinions. Teach me to walk in humility and boldness at the same time.
Let my life be a bridge between heaven's justice and earth's brokenness.

Raise me up to defend the vulnerable, to protect the unseen, to love the unloved, and to restore dignity to the forgotten.
Let me speak up when silence is safe.
Let me stand when standing is costly.
Let me serve when it's inconvenient because that's the way of Jesus.

Lord, I pray for systems to be healed, for wrongs to be made right, and for those in power to fear You above all.
Let justice roll down like a mighty river, and righteousness flow like an unending stream.
Raise up voices of truth, hearts of mercy, and hands that heal.

When I grow weary, remind me that You are the God who fights for the oppressed and walks with the brokenhearted.

Use my prayers to shift atmospheres.
Use my hands to carry hope.
Use my life to glorify You.

In the mighty name of Jesus who stood with the broken, touched the unclean, and laid down His life for all, Amen.

Declaration of Faith and Truth

"I am a vessel of God's justice, love, and mercy. I will not close my eyes to the hurting or silence my voice in the face of injustice. I am called, equipped, and positioned to reflect His heart on the earth."

Faith in Action

Who in your community or in the world is hurting, overlooked, or in need of advocacy? How can you bring justice or mercy to that situation through prayer, giving, or personal involvement?

Faith in Action Response

_____
_____
_____
_____
_____
_____
_____
_____
_____
_____
_____
_____

Act of Gratitude

Write down one thing you're grateful for today that connects with the focus of your prayer.

_____
_____
_____
_____

Things to Remember

_____
_____
_____
_____
_____
_____
_____
_____
_____

Faith for Generations to Come

Scripture Meditation

"But from everlasting to everlasting the Lord's love is with those who fear him, and his righteousness with their children's children."
–Psalm 103:17 (NIV)

"One generation will commend your works to another; they will tell of your mighty acts."
–Psalm 145:4 (NIV)

Reflection

God is a generational God. His promises extend beyond your lifetime, reaching into the lives of your children, grandchildren, and spiritual descendants. Your faith is never just about you. It is a seed with the power to bless those who come after you.

Whether you are raising children, mentoring others, or praying for family members yet to be born, your prayers help build a spiritual foundation that can outlast the present moment. The way you seek God today can become a testimony, a covering, and a legacy for others tomorrow.

Even if your family history feels marked by brokenness, you have the authority in Christ to start a new chapter. You are not bound to the past. You are chosen to pass down faith and blessing. What you plant in prayer today, God can multiply across generations.

Bold Prayer for Faith for Generations to Come

Heavenly Father,
Thank You for being faithful through all generations.

Today, I lift up the ones who will come after me. I pray for my children, grandchildren, and spiritual sons and daughters.

Cover them with Your presence. Draw them close to You. Let my life point them toward Christ, not just with words but with love, obedience, and faith.

Where past generations have left wounds or brokenness, I ask You to bring healing and restoration. Let my home be marked by blessing, peace, and Your presence.

I trust You to finish what You've started and to write a legacy that brings You glory. In Jesus' Name, Amen.

Declaration of Faith and Truth

"My prayers today shape tomorrow. I am building a legacy of faith, blessing, and obedience. God's promises will not end with me; they will echo through generations to come."

Faith in Action (Journal Prompt)

What legacy of faith do you want to leave behind? Write a prayer, blessing, or declaration over someone in the next generation by name, if possible.

Faith in Action Response

_____
_____
_____
_____
_____
_____
_____
_____
_____
_____

Act of Gratitude

Write down one thing you're grateful for today that connects with the focus of your prayer.

_____
_____
_____
_____

Things to Remember

_____
_____
_____
_____
_____
_____
_____
_____

Summary of the Prayer Themes

1. Faith & Confidence
2. Provision & Financial Breakthrough
3. Healing & Restoration
4. Spiritual Growth & Intimacy with God
5. Purpose & Direction
6. Family & Relationships
7. Forgiveness & Freedom
8. Protection & Spiritual Warfare
9. Peace, Rest & Joy
10. Hope & Future Promise
11. Obedience & Discipline
12. Wisdom & Discernment
13. Calling & Ministry
14. Unity in the Body of Christ
15. Identity & Worth in Christ
16. Patience & Perseverance
17. Creative Expression & Kingdom Innovation
18. Time & Priorities
19. Emotional Healing & Wholeness
20. Justice, Mercy & the Marginalized
21. Faith for Generations to Come

Conclusion: This Is Just the Beginning

If you've reached this point and you have done the work, something in you has already changed.

You've prayed boldly. You've listened for God's voice. You've opened your heart to His power, His presence, and His promises, and that kind of pursuit never ends the same way it started.

Now that you are here, hopefully, you have found this journey of 21 prayers to be more than just a devotional, and more of **an awakening**.

It was about shaking off timidity and stepping into authority. About releasing old patterns and walking in divine purpose. About learning not just to pray, but to **pray like someone who knows God is listening,** because He is.

As you close this book, know this:

You are not done.

You are being launched.

This is not the finish line; it's the foundation because a life of bold prayer is a life that stays open, alert, and expectant.
It's not a moment you had; it's now a lifestyle you carry.

Keep praying.

Keep declaring.

Keep standing on His Word.

Let the Holy Spirit continue to grow you in strength, clarity, and courage. Let your faith rise higher than your fear. Let your voice echo what heaven is already saying.

And remember this:
God didn't bring you through this journey just to inspire you. He brought you here to **ignite you.**

The world needs your fire. The Church needs your voice.
And your future is waiting for your faith.

Stay bold. Stay surrendered and above all, stay close to the One who answers.

With faith and fire,
Caleb Elias Hart

Notes and Reflections

www.ingramcontent.com/pod-product-compliance
Lightning Source LLC
Chambersburg PA
CBHW050647160426
43194CB00010B/1844